Helpful Hints and Guidelines to Successful Painting

Jerome Thompson

ISBN 978-1-64468-008-7 (Paperback)
ISBN 978-1-64468-009-4 (Digital)

Covenant Books, Inc.
11661 Hwy 707
Murrells Inlet, SC 29576
www.covenantbooks.com

This book is dedicated to all beginner and future artists… For them I comprised this book.

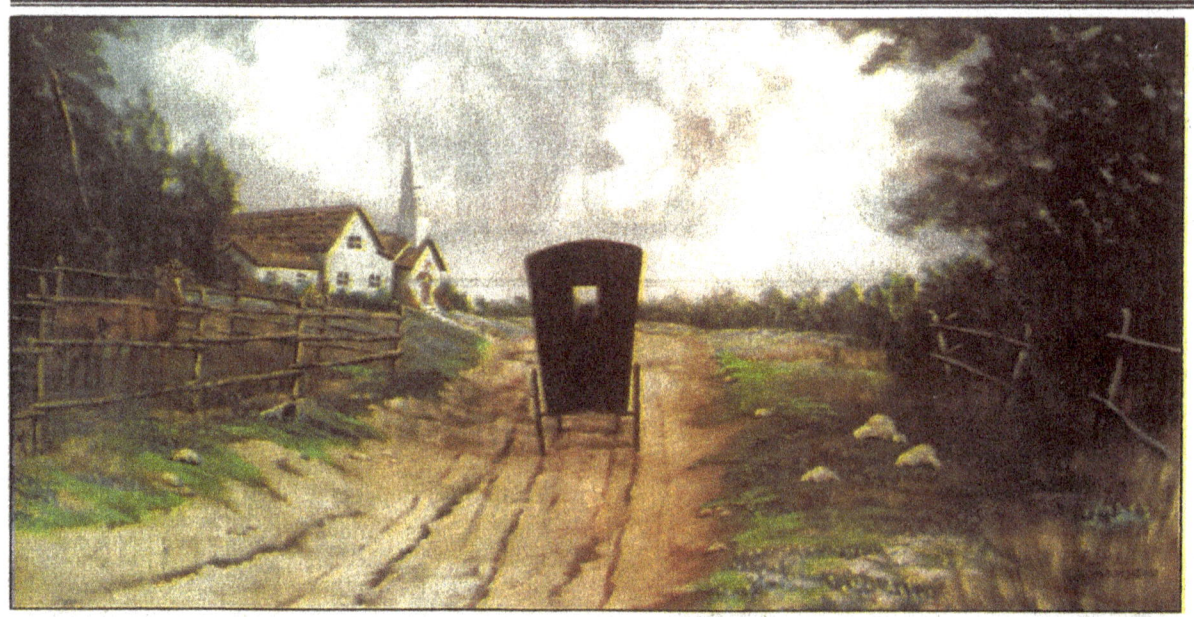

Local artist Jerome Thompson creates charming country landscapes like the one shown above. His work will be displayed at The Color of Ideas Community Arts Center in Athens.

The Color of Ideas

Local artist displays at community arts center

By Philokalia Jones

Local artist Jerome Thompson took his first painting class long ago and far away -- back in the 1970s.

From then until now, painting has always been an important part of Jerome's life. Even in retirement, Jerome continues to paint with skill and remarkable focus.

"When I paint I go at it for seven or eight hours at a time," he said.

Charming country landscapes, Western themes and cozy cottages are some of Jerome's favorite subjects.

The Color of Ideas Community Arts Center, located just east of the square at 207 E. Tyler St., is currently showing a major exhibit of Jerome's work. Professionally-matted and framed by Athens' own Frame House, Jerome's work will appeal to a broad range of people.

In addition to showing his remarkable artwork at The Color of Ideas (TCOI), Jerome is starting up a Beginner's Painting Class at TCOI next Saturday, Beginning Feb. 1.

Jerome's 20-week class will run from 1 p.m. until 4 p.m. The class will require considerable commitment of time. The class cost is $20 for a 3-hour class.

Supplies will cost anywhere from $50 to $100, depending on the quality of materials selected.

At present, four people are enrolled in the class, leaving room for two more people. If there is enough interest, a second class will be formed.

Jerome's claim is that anyone who finishes his 20-week course will have the confidence to paint virtually anything they like.

Sign up by stopping by The Color of Ideas, or calling Jerome directly at 214 399-6036 for more details.

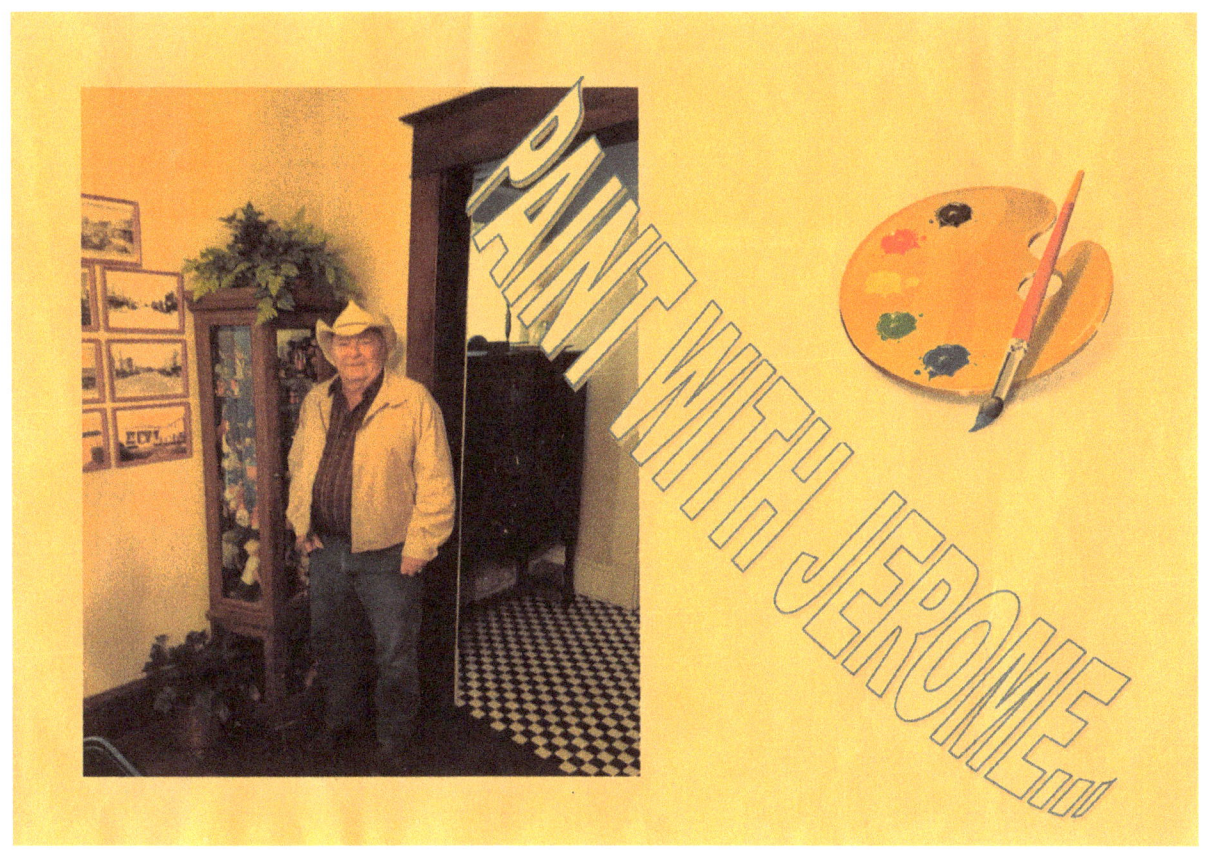

After thirty-five years of successful painting, I wanted to share my knowledge and answer some of the questions you will have as a beginner. These hints took me many years to learn. I hope this book of helpful hints and guidelines to successful painting will help you along the way.

Happy painting.

Jerome Thompson, 2012

GUIDELINE 1

Suggestion: artist option
Hint: Use Masters (brand name, Touch)
    140 lb cold-pressed surface acid free watercolor paper, twelve-sheet book
    Why? Less expensive than canvas, works great with acrylics, fast to paint on, size preference.

BEGINNERS' LESSON 1

1. What to paint?
   a. Choose subjects that you like.
   b. Choose subjects that are interesting.
   c. Think décor for wall hanging.
      1) Do not get hung up on one size.
      2) Consider mattes and framing.
   d. All subjects are not necessarily printable or make a pretty painting.
   e. Keep as simple as possible.
2. Where to get subjects?*
   a. Take photos
   b. Magazines
   c. Do your own sketches
   d. Art books
   e. Postcards

f. What colors?

a. All color spectrum, if there is a good balance of color.

    1) I have found that choosing your colors has a lot to do with what mood you are in. You have heard of moody artists. It does reflect in your paintings.

b. Experiment—all colors or natural to the eye, considering darks, lights, and their values

c. Choose colors that are pleasing to you.

    1) You are the artist. You are in control. Please yourself first.

*Note: All successful artists use a visual subject to paint by. Do not try to paint just out of your head despite what you have heard as beginners.

BEGINNERS' LESSON 2

You Are Ready to Start

1. But where do you start?
   a. Always start with the sky.
      1) Choose the sky colors carefully (remember moods) because the sky will determine the mood and theme of your painting.
      2) Why? Your sky always reflects the contentions of the weather and seasons of mood and colors just like you can tell when you look outside.

2. Sky colors will always have an influence of colors throughout your paintings.

a. Why? Because all natural colors reflect light that produces different values of your primary colors.

b. Examples:

   1) Light warm sky = light warm values

   2) Dark moody sky = dark to medium values

   3) Morning sky = vibrant values, yellows, blues

   4) Evening sky = vibrant values, reds, oranges, blues

BEGINNERS' LESSON 3

Reflected Light

1. Again: mood of sky colors
   a. Sets mood of painting
      Examples:
      1) Summer
      2) Winter
      3) Fall
      4) Spring
      5) Evening
      6) Morning
      7) Stormy
      8) Warm
2. Everything doesn't have a natural color.
   a. Water

1) Always use sky colors, reflected colors.
2) Why? Because the only color water will get is reflected from sky, trees, rocks, grass, etc. *Note: As a general law of painting use lighter values to show light, darker to medium values for shadows and depth. You can only get 25 percent projection of natural light in painting, so you must play heavy on lights and darks.

b. Snow
1) Same rules apply.

c. Mountains
1) Same rules apply.
2) Why? Because most mountains are painted as a background, at a distance haze, or atmosphere.
3) Again sky colors play a major part according to the moods and colors of mountains and reflections.
*Note: Rule—use sky color mixed in different values with primary colors to create

distance and reflected light to give your mountains a natural look. I have found that Payne's gray ultra-marine blue mixed with white creates a good distant mountain color.

d. Trees

   1) Yes, even though trees do have a natural color, sky light plays a major role.

      a. Again, to show high light lights sky colors mixed with primary colors in much lighter values.

      b. Consider light direction for lights on primary tree, leaves, branches, etc. Primary meaning for ground.

c. Clouds

   1) Yes, because the only color clouds have is reflected from sky color and the sun.

   2) Rule—sky color mixed to create clouds with white or lighter values in the same color spectrum

3) Darks mixed with sky colors such as gray, black, greens, etc.
4) Remember your sky and trees are a natural part of your painting so you want to make them as interesting as you can.

3. Balance

a. A good painting should have a good balance of color. Lights and darks.

b. Remember you cannot show light without darks, so you can not show light without a light source direction that will result in shadows and shade.

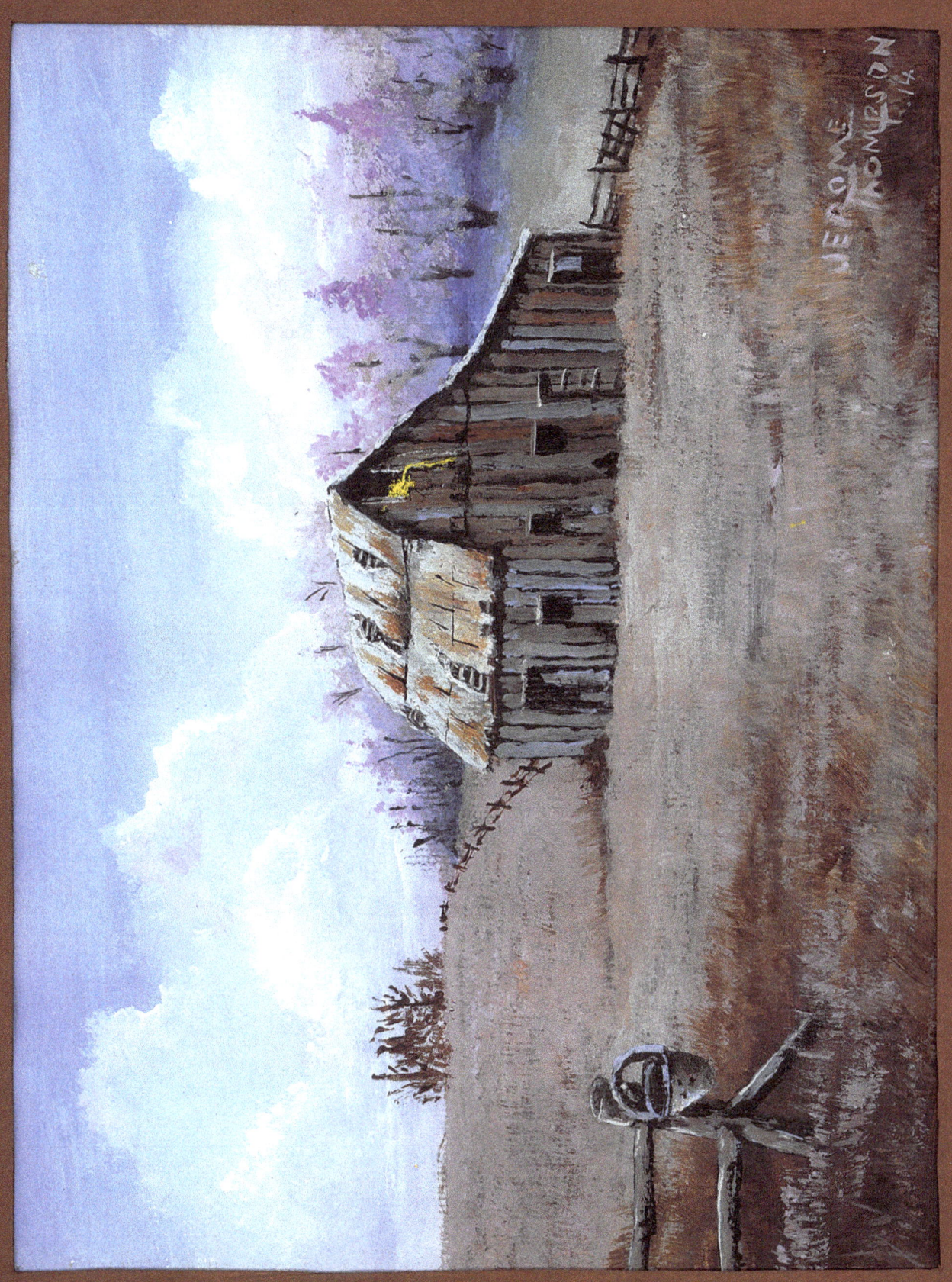

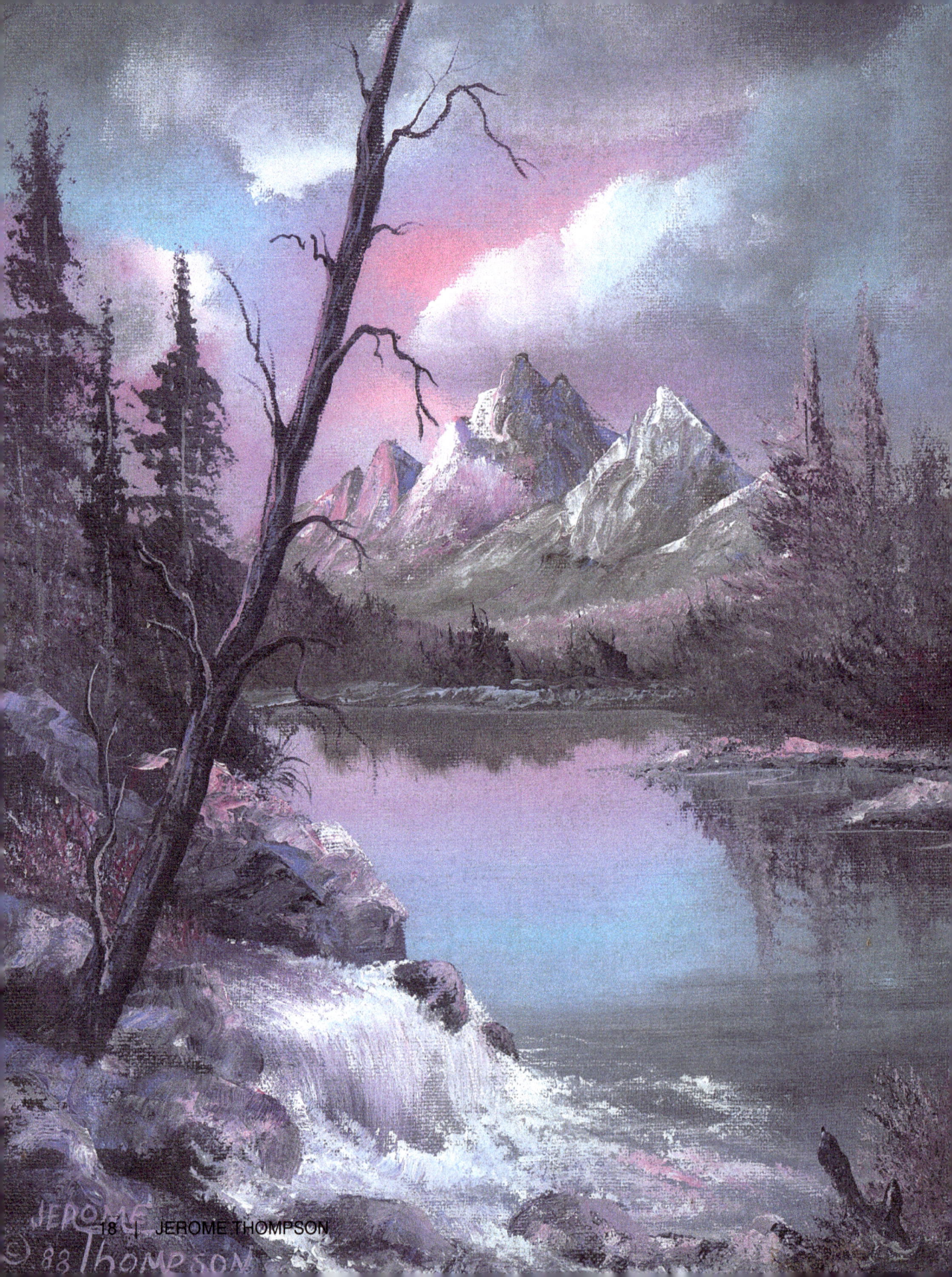

JEROME Thompson
© 88

Example:

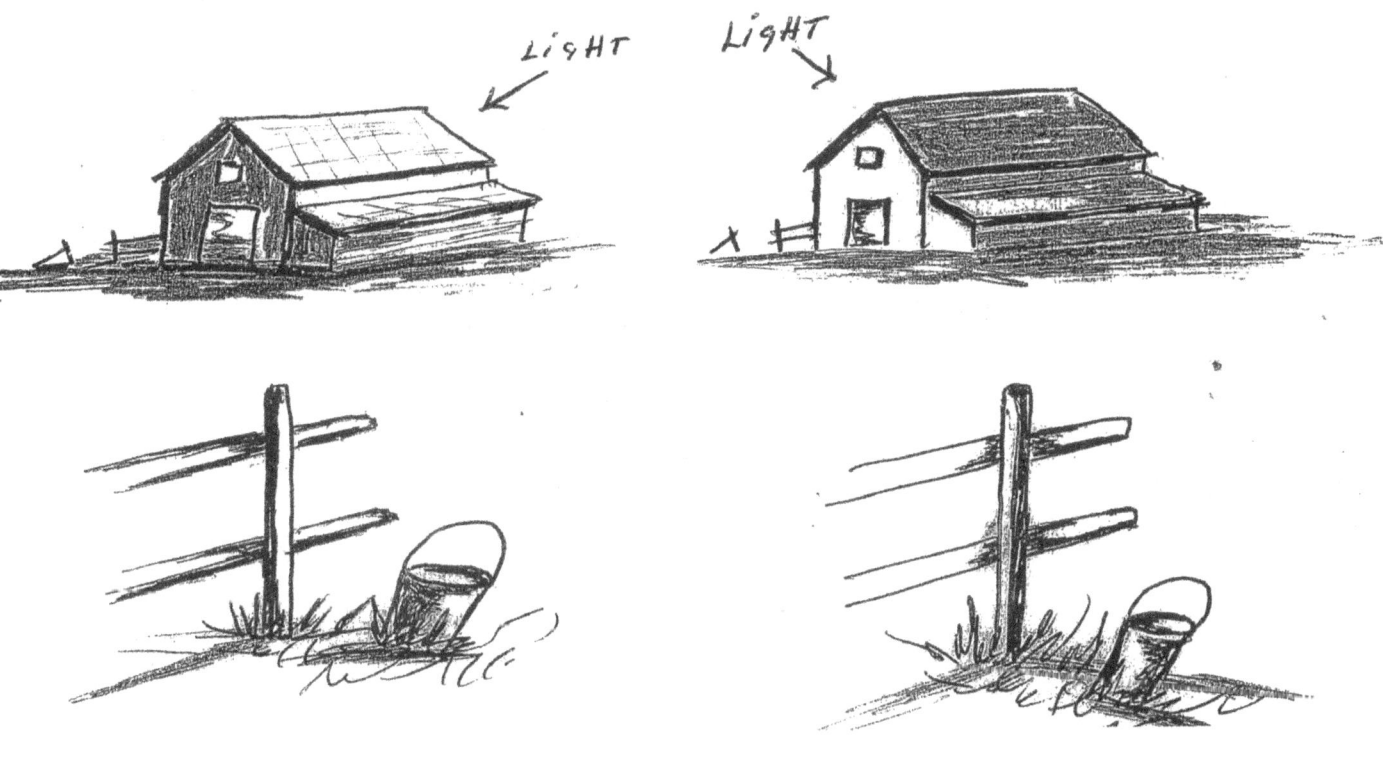

**Rule—do not be afraid to show contrast
in light to dark values according
to light source. *Think light.***

BEGINNERS' LESSON 4

Prospective Balance

1. Composition Balance
   a. A good painting should be well balanced to your main vocal point.
      1) Keep your main subject in view.
      2) Do not clutter your painting with too much of what is not necessary.
      3) Keep your depth in good prospective balance.

      Examples: wrong and right

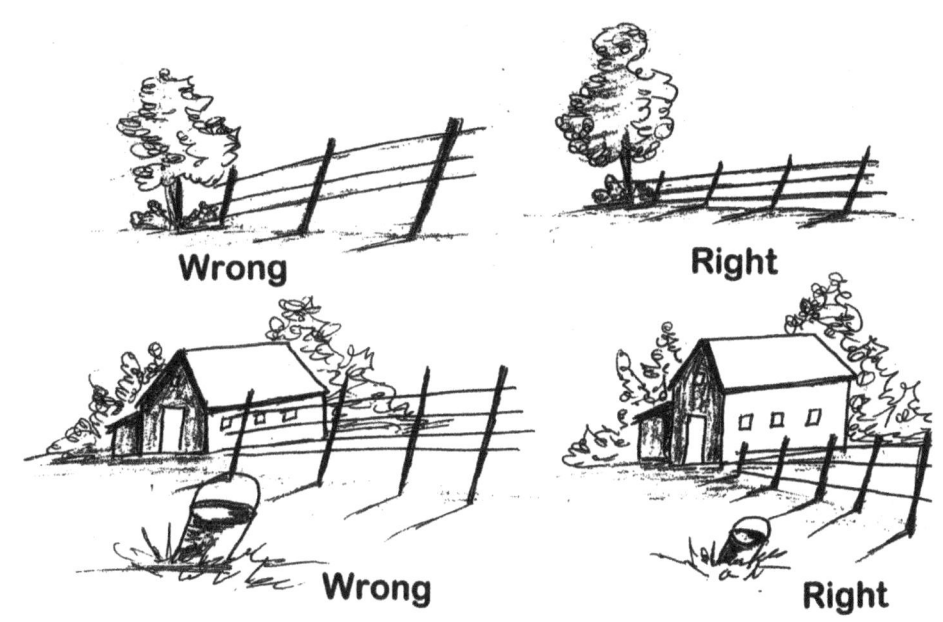

Wrong

Right

Wrong

Right

Rule: Do not overpower your painting with too much to look at. Keep it as simple as possible with prospective balance.

Guideline: refer to Lesson 2 and 3

Hints: Commonly used to enhance interest in middle and foreground signs of life activity.

Mountain	Barns
1. Lake	1. Loft, hay
2. Reflections	2. Water barrels
3. Boats, piers	3. Old buckets
4. Flying ducks	4. Rail post, gates, fence

| 5. Birds, trees | 5. Rocks, paths, roads, trees |

Use inspiration to country mailboxes, whatever subject will support. Rule calls for artist inspiration for visual interest.

Hint: First glance matters. It is very important to catch people's eye from across the room of subject interest.

BEGINNERS' LESSON 5

Artist Pallet

1. What colors do I need?
   a. You must have a standard color pallet for landscape painting.
   (Note: I recommend Liquitex Acrylic Paints (2 oz tubes) for good color consistency tube to tube.)
   b. There are only three phases in landscape painting
      1. Background—keep it interesting (very important); show atmosphere: clouds, mountains, distant trees, etc.
      2. Middle ground—use good perspective

3. Foreground—paint with detail to subject of painting

c. Refer to Lesson 2 and 3 guidelines.

ens Daily Review is committed to serving Henderson County five days a
lews brief or idea, email editor Chad Wilson at editor@athensreview.com

Beginners acrylic painting class

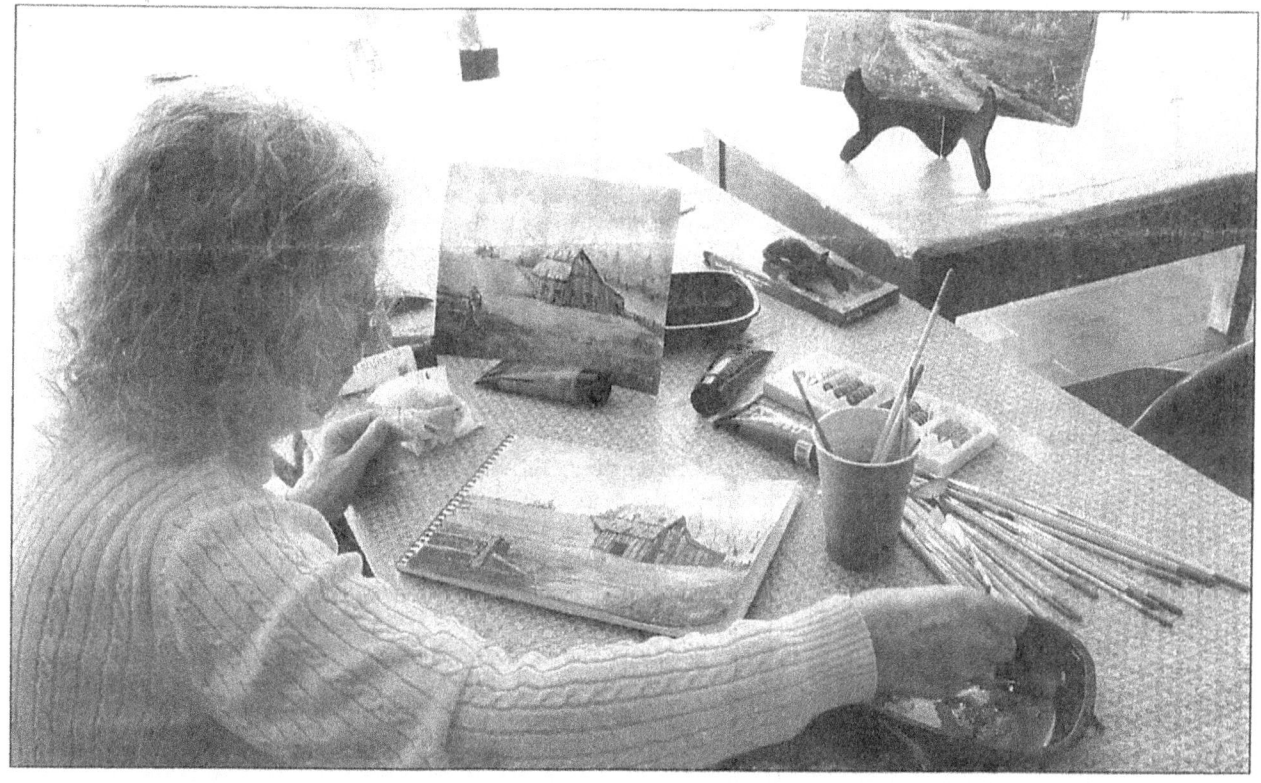

The Color of Ideas Community Arts Center (TCOI), located just off the Square at 207 E. Tyler St., announces a new Beginners Acrylic Painting Class. Led by local artist Jerome Thompson, the new class will meet every week from noon to 3 p.m., beginning on Thursday, Oct. 18. Weekly cost for the 3-hour class is only $20. If there is interest, a second class will be organized for Saturday. Enrollment is open, meaning you can join the class any time throughout the coming year. No painting experience is needed at all. Cost of supplies, enough to last for months, is under $30. If you are looking for something new and fun to do, don't miss this opportunity to learn how to paint, and make new friends at the same time. To sign up, or ask questions, call 903-880-3995, or drop by TCOI Tuesday through Saturday, from 9 a.m. to noon.

BEGINNERS' LESSON 6

Artist Pallet

1. Suggested color pallet for landscape painting can be added to as need for color value (light and shadows).

   (Note: White or black used to change value of color 4 oz tube suggested)

   a. Background—basic
      1) Cearean blue
      2) Ultra-marie blue
      3) Cobalt blue
      4) Light blue violet
   b. Earth tones—basic
      1) Burnt umber—4 oz tube
      2) Burnt sienna

3) Raw sienna
4) Raw umber
5) Payne's gray
6) Red oxide

c. Foreground—basic
1) Hooker's green—4 oz tube
2) Chromium green
3) Light emerald green
4) Yellow light hansa
5) Naples yellow
6) Prism violet
7) Light violet permanent
8) Light oxide green

2. Colors to enhance pallet
a. Hues and value colors of all color wheel spectrum of colors
b. Folk Art (brand) acrylic paint
1) All colors of value
2) 2 oz bottles
   (Note: Used mostly for tole painting but great for value colors)

BEGINNERS' LESSON 7

What Kind of Brushes Do I Need?

1. A variety of types and sizes are needed for different aspects of your painting (large, medium, small).

   (Note: I have found that bristle brushes work best with acrylic paint)

   a. Variety 5—pack bristle brushes
   b. 2 large brushes—1/2"–1"
   c. 2 liner brushes—medium/fine
   d. No. 4 fan brush bristle
   e. Small fan brush
   f. Variety of brushes medium to small
   g. Pallet knife

2. Helpful aides to help with your painting composition
   a. 12" ruler
   b. Charcoal sticks—soft
   c. Sharpe Brand Ultra Fine Point
      (Note: Paper towels and used large coffee can lid as a pallet)

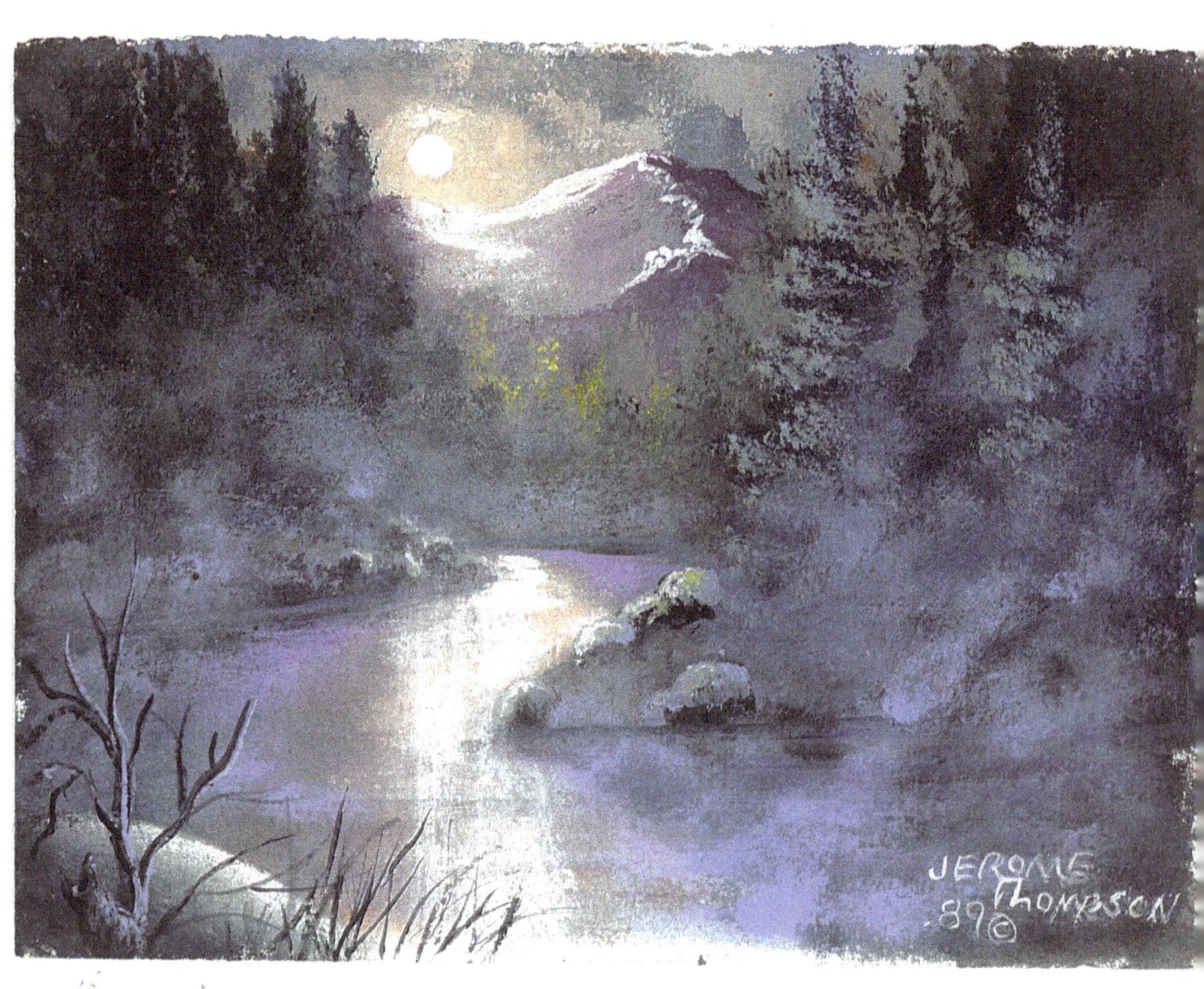

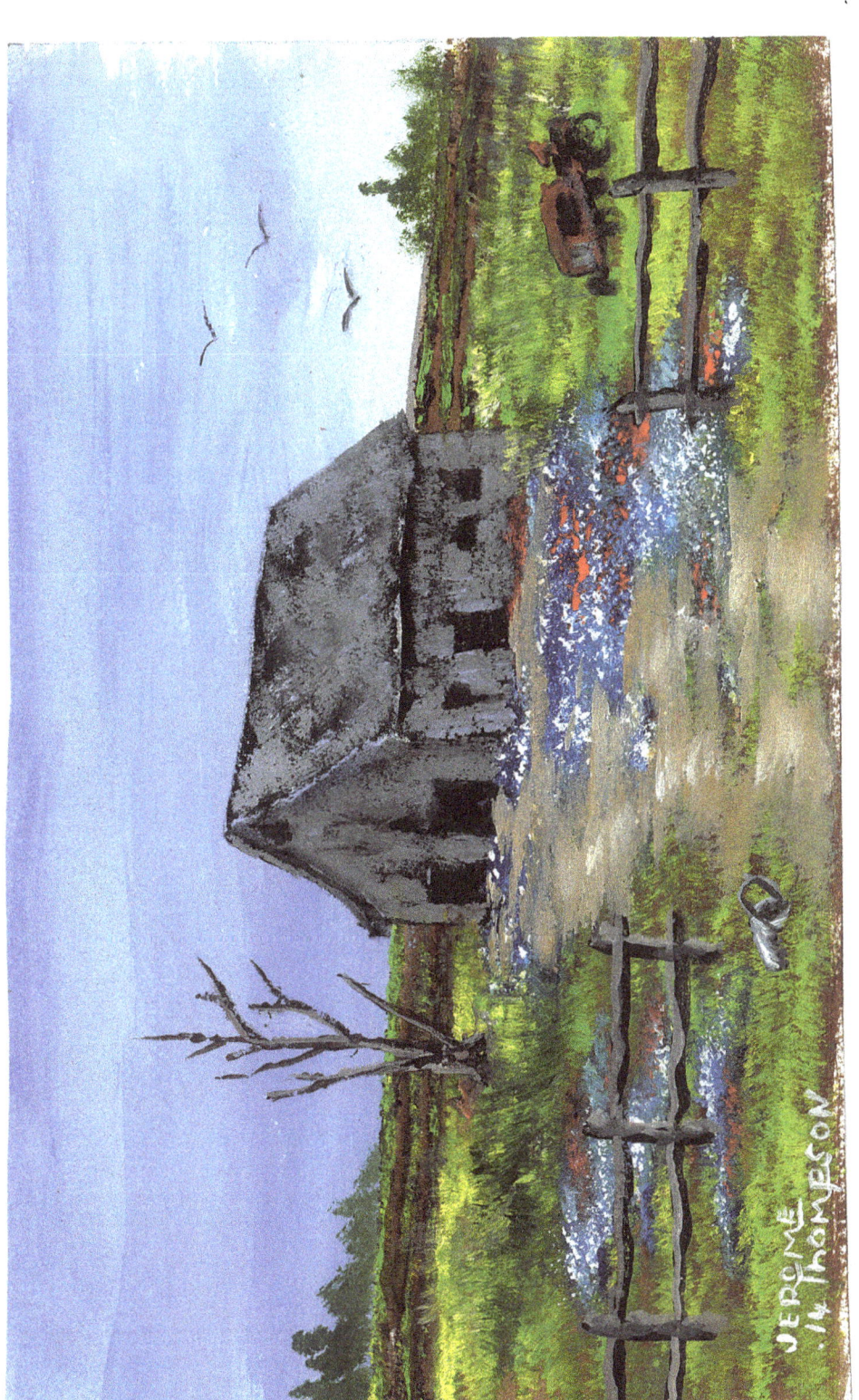

FOREGOTEN BARN

JEROME
.14 THOMPSON

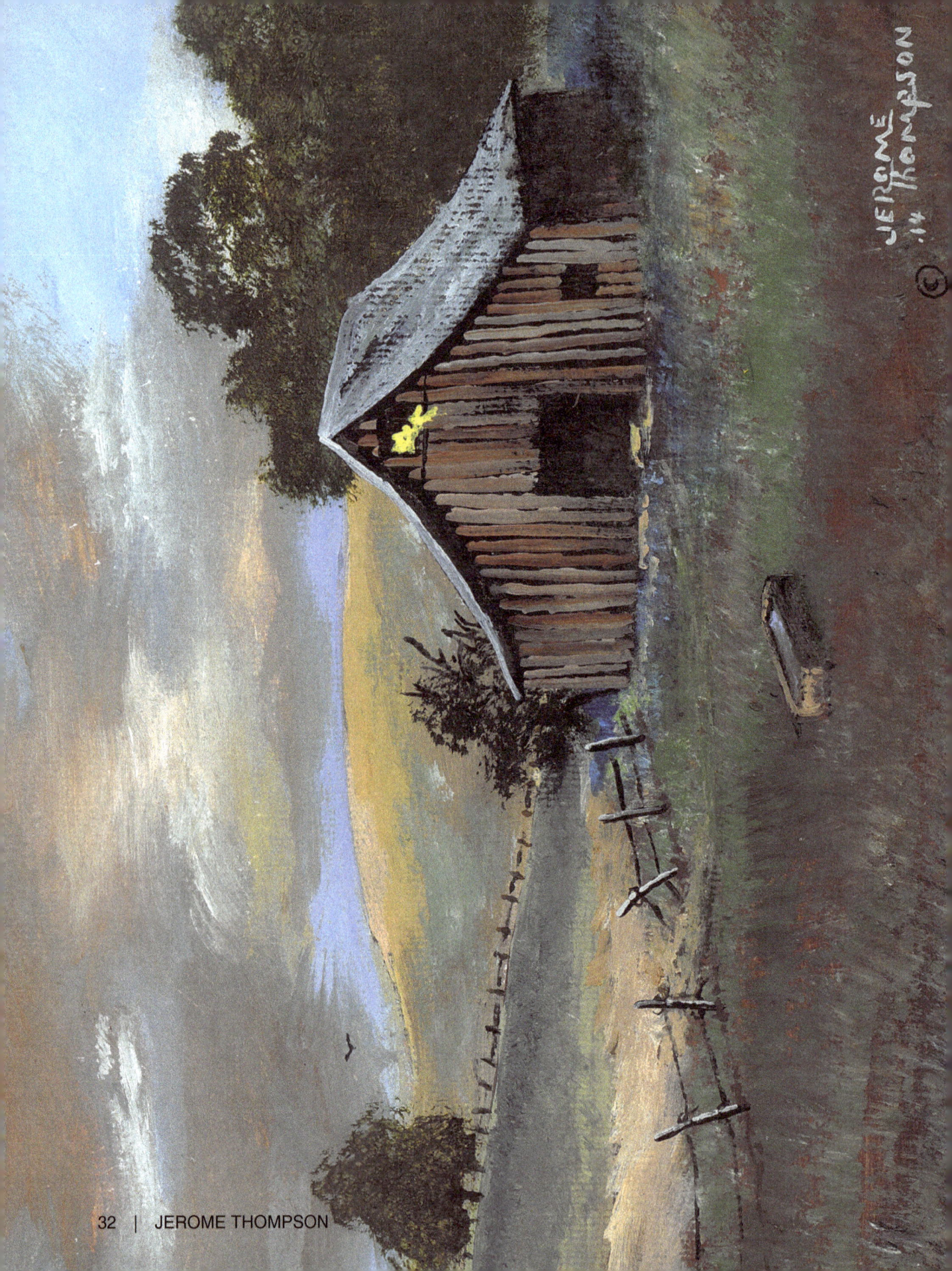

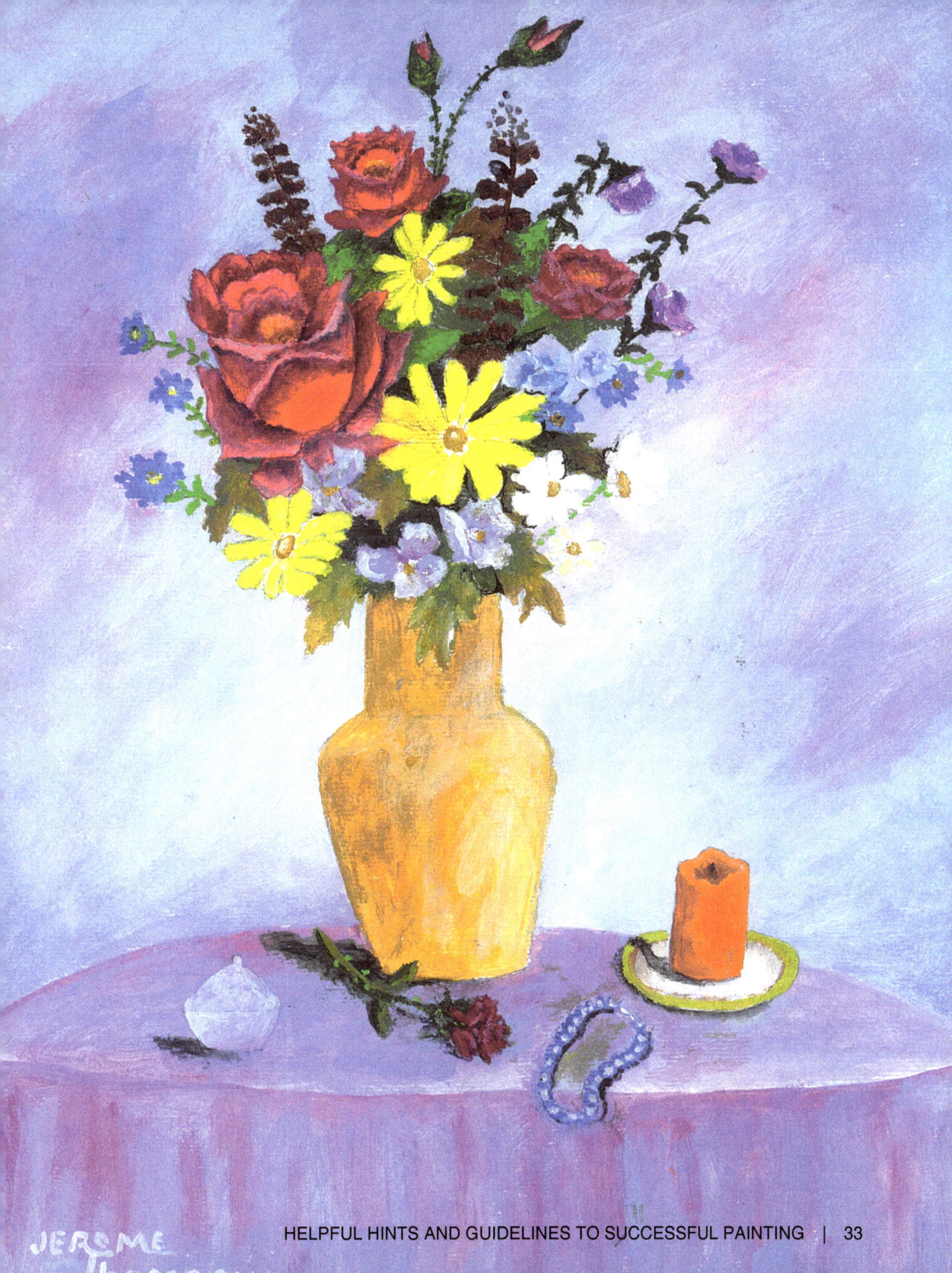

ABOUT THE AUTHOR

Jerome Thompson has been a successful painter for thirty-five years. One of his pleasures and desires in life was to teach students to paint. He fulfilled that dream and taught for thirty plus years. He has been married to his wife, Linda, for sixty-one years. When asked about his painting, she said that she would wake up to him painting until the early hours of the morning. After suffering a stroke, Jerome can no longer paint but wants to share all his tips and tricks he has learned throughout the years with the world!

Thank you.

Remember, you can't paint without paint and everything you paint shows a color, so don't be afraid to use color to enhance your work.

Happy painting.

Jerome Thompson, 2012

www.ingramcontent.com/pod-product-compliance
Lightning Source LLC
Chambersburg PA
CBHW041922180526
45172CB00013B/1356